W9-CDX-594

CHILL

Discover the Cool (and Creative) Side of Your Fridge

WRITTEN BY ALLAN PETERKIN
ILLUSTRATED BY MIKE SHIELL

Kids Can Press

Text © 2009 Allan Peterkin
Illustrations © 2009 Mike Shiell

Kids Can Press acknowledges the financial support of the Government of Ontario, through the Ontario Media Development Corporation's Ontario Book Initiative; the Ontario Arts Council; the Canada Council for the Arts; and the Government of Canada, through the BPIDP, for our publishing activity.

Published in Canada by
Kids Can Press Ltd.
29 Birch Avenue
Toronto, ON M4V 1E2

Published in the U.S. by
Kids Can Press Ltd.
2250 Military Road
Tonawanda, NY 14150

www.kidscanpress.com

Edited by Sheila Barry and Samantha Swenson
Designed by Marie Bartholomew
Printed and bound in Singapore

The paper used to print this book was produced with elemental chlorine-free pulp harvested from managed sustainable forests.

The hardcover edition of this book is smyth sewn casebound.
The paperback edition of this book is limp sewn with a drawn-on cover.

CM 09 0 9 8 7 6 5 4 3 2 1
CM PA 09 0 9 8 7 6 5 4 3 2 1

Library and Archives Canada Cataloguing in Publication

Peterkin, Allan D.
      Chill: discover the cool (and creative) side of your fridge / Allan
Peterkin ; Mike Shiell, [illustrator].

ISBN 978-1-55453-429-6 (bound) ISBN 978-1-55453-301-5 (pbk.)

1. Refrigerators — Juvenile literature. 2. Handicraft — Juvenile literature.
I. Shiell, Mike II. Title.

TT160.P468 2009   j745.5   C2008-903976-9

Kids Can Press is a *l©rUS*™ Entertainment company

C·O·N·T·E·N·T·S

4

Why Fridge Art?

Before you immerse yourself in this book, take a few minutes to ask yourself the following extremely important questions — and then read the answers that the author of this book has kindly provided.

Q: What kind of moron would write a whole book on the subject of fridge art?

A: Resistance is futile. With minimal effort, I will convince you that the refrigerator is the center of your family's universe. Think about it. You can probably imagine a week without computers or television — not the best week of your life, maybe, but your father is right that it wouldn't kill you. Now try to imagine a week without food. Your fridge feeds you three times a day (more if you're a compulsive snacker). In fact, a family of four typically visits the fridge eleven times per day (not including holidays). You do the math, smarty-pants. That's a minimum of 16 000 visits per year! That's right, your refrigerator is your best friend.

Q: Okay, I should be grateful for my refrigerator. So what?

A: Forgive me for answering your question with more questions, but I think you might be missing the point here. Sure, your fridge feeds you, and that's great. But what else can it do for you? What if your fridge could make your spare time more interesting? Make your family more functional? Give you a sense of artistic accomplishment? Maybe even make you some extra cash? Oh, yes, now I have your attention!

Q: Can your book really do all these things? I have my doubts.

A: You have doubts, but I have experts. Just turn the page to read their testimonials. Then turn the next page, and the one after that, and keep turning until you reach the end of the book. You will learn how to decorate your fridge with hundreds of objects. You will develop special occasion and theme fridges. You will learn the advanced techniques that will help you become a fridge art consultant. Congratulations! Your life is about to change forever.

What Is Fridge Art?

We asked those who make and study
it, and here's what they had to say:

"Your fridge is like a Christmas tree that never dies. You can just
keep decorating it, and it won't shed."

— *Lucretia, serial fridge decorator*

"Sticking rubber snakes to the fridge is a perfect way
to annoy my big sister."

— *Leonard, devious sibling*

"The refrigerator is like a changeable graffiti wall — that won't get you arrested."

— *Ice-T-Cool, stay-at-home graffiti guy*

"Fridge art takes a cold metal fridge and makes it warm and personal."

— *Aunt Louise*

"The fridge door is a bulletin board minus the thumbtacks."

— *accident-prone office worker*

"It's a cheap way to cover scratches and dents on our old fridge."

— *lazy dad*

"My fridge reminds me, every morning, of my current infatuations with people, places and things."

— *Paris Stilton, cheesy starlet*

"A blank fridge is the sign of a lazy mind."

— *Zack Zed, creativity coach*

"Every time I get expelled, putting up the fridge magnets in my new dorm room makes it feel like home."

— *Ned, boarding school reject*

Factoid

Thirty percent of the cold air escapes each time you open the fridge door (which is why we all stand there on hot days).

Quiz: Celebrity Fridges

Match the refrigerator to
its famous owner.

1. Cleopatra
2. Einstein
3. Houdini
4. Napoleon
5. Picasso

(Answers on page 78)

PART ONE

HISTORY

(or "the origins of all things fridgely and creative")

d

e

A Brief History of Refrigeration

You open it a dozen times a day ... but do you really *know* your refrigerator? How it works? Where it came from? Who its ancestors were? No? Well, here's an ultra-condensed history of chilling.

It all started because humans need to eat. Food goes bad. Put it all together and you have cavemen figuring out that brontosaurus steaks don't smell as gross when they are kept in the coolest part of the cave.

By 1000 B.C.E., the Chinese were using ice cut from the hills for food storage. The Greeks and Romans stored ice in shallow, straw-lined pits — basically they had horizontal, dug-out fridges rather than stands-ups.

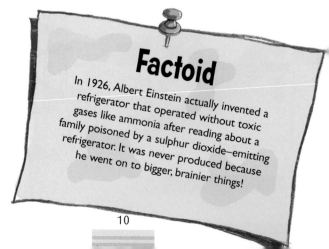

Factoid

In 1926, Albert Einstein actually invented a refrigerator that operated without toxic gases like ammonia after reading about a family poisoned by a sulphur dioxide—emitting refrigerator. It was never produced because he went on to bigger, brainier things!

What if you didn't have access to seasonal snow or icy mountaintops? By 500 B.C.E., the Egyptians were making ice blocks by leaving clay pots of water outdoors on cold nights.

After that, not much happened for about 2000 years until the 1550s, when the Italians figured out that adding certain chemicals like sodium nitrate or potassium nitrate to water would lower its temperature to create a "refrigeration bath"— perfect for chilling their wine.

By the 1700s, rich people in England started building icehouses on their estates. Mitten-clad servants gathered ice during winter months and stored the blocks for use in summer. All this so the boss could sip frosty lemonade in June and not break a sweat.

But the biggest breakthrough was yet to come …

Refrigeration!

TV DINNER TIME, SON

People got busy in the 1800s and experimented with all kinds of refrigeration techniques.

First, a vapor-compression system, which is where hot, compressed vapor is condensed, leading to cooling. Then came a system that used ammonia, which was great if you didn't mind the potential hazard of stinky gas leaking out. But these were mostly for industrial use. At home, people still just used the icebox idea from the 1700s — just in a more compact container (a wooden cabinet with drawers to hold the ice).

In 1870, German engineer Carl von Linde, the granddaddy of modern refrigeration, developed and patented a process for industrial cooling that combined all of the principles of gas compression. His patents eventually became the model for the household fridge we know, love and decorate today.

But even this new model was still hazardous, due to the type of gases that were used: ammonia (again), sulphur dioxide and methyl chloride. Yuck!

Enter Freon, an odorless, non-toxic gas invented in the 1920s that could be used in smaller units better suited for home use. (Sadly, no one realized that over time, Freon and similar fridge gases would eat a hole in the ozone layer.)

By 1925, steel cabinets started replacing wood-framed fridges and were thought to be very high-tech and glamorous. In 1939, the first refrigerator with two compartments — one on top for freezing and one on the bottom for chilling — appeared on the American market.

Fancy accessories like egg holders, removable grill shelving and door racks for bottles had become a must for the modern kitchen by 1946.

Factoid

The first ice cube tray appeared in a 1914 fridge as a built-in tray. Modern flexible ice cube trays like we use today were invented by Guy L. Tinkham in 1933.

Ornate fridge magnets started appearing on store shelves and fridge doors by the 1960s, unleashing a FRIDGE ART CRAZE that has never slowed down. (See Lady Sibyl Snivel's highly polished history of this art form on page 14.)

Where Did Fridge Art Come From?

or "Give Them a Blank Space and They Will Fill It"

by Lady Sibyl Snivel, the British Institute of Refrigerative Expression

When prehistoric cave drawings were first discovered, we learned how humans lived long ago. My fellow historians have made a big to-do about pictures of hunting, gathering, etc., but what they fail to realize is that these charming little markings are, in fact, the first evidence of what we now call fridge art. Clearly, caves were cool and our hairy ancestors stored foodstuffs in them to avoid spoiling. No doubt, they got chatting while admiring the beasts they had slaughtered and cut into chops and started doodling on the walls to record their exploits. In my favorite example, one fellow—Urgg, as I shall call him—demonstrates that the brontosaurus he caught is bigger than that of his neighbor's. We see flowers at the very bottom of the drawing—no doubt added by his children, given the low positioning and use of color.

Thereafter, we can see the emergence of graffiti as artistic human expression in all eras. My own highly controversial theory is that fridge art is itself a kind of graffiti. Do read on ...

Fridge art as we know it today first appeared when steel cabinets began to replace wooden iceboxes. Steel, whether silver or white, simply begged to be adorned. According to legend, in 1930 little Eleanor Frigg, a five year old from Brooklyn, fastened one of her drawings to the metal fridge door with a piece of chewing gum. There was no turning back. Her brother Frank took a small magnet from his science set and stuck it to one of his own drawings of a fire truck. Thus began a creative rivalry that lasted all their lives. Both have written memoirs claiming to be the first to start the modern fridge art movement. It is true that Frank's method of hanging art has endured better than his sister's, but she was first …

A man called Zimmerman claims to have patented the first fridge magnet in the 1970s, but we have been unable to substantiate this claim. And, anyway, we know Eleanor and Frank beat him to it.

It wasn't untill decades after the Friggs that the emergence of plastic and other synthetic substances allowed for the cheap production of amusing magnet shapes in an endless number of themes. Fridge magnets spread like a plague, and the metal refrigerator was permanently transformed. It became a family picture album, a rotating exhibition for youthful crayonists, a memo holder extraordinaire. The cold cuts inside the icebox had clearly become secondary to the messages conveyed on the door.

Factoid

Popsicles were invented in 1905 by eleven-year-old Frank Epperson when he left a fruit drink and straw on the front porch overnight. The temperature dropped, and in the morning Frank pulled out a tasty treat. In 1923, Frank obtained a patent for his invention, changing the name from Epsicle to Popsicle.

The advent of new adhesives — tape, stickers, putty — as well as more powerful magnets has allowed for even greater artistic experimentation. Almost anything can now be stuck to the fridge door. Somewhere along the line, adults got in on the act, but practical items like dental appointment cards can hardly be called art. Like Urgg's offspring, young people have tended to be more playful, creative and innovative. The future of fridge art is safe in their capable hands.

Quiz: What's Inside the Fridge?

Match the contents of the fridge to the person.

1. Type A, B and AB blood (no garlic)

2. Sour milk, rotten eggs and an onion

3. A bowl of fruit marked "Do not touch!"

4. A mayo-covered sandwich-bread log house with olive windows and a pickle chimney

5. Cans of tuna, jugs of cream and sacks of catnip

6. Nothing but carrots and iceberg lettuce

7. Three hundred and forty-six packets of mustard, ketchup, vinegar, soy sauce and sugar

a. Someone with no sense of smell

b. A frustrated architect

c. A rabbit

d. A restaurant kleptomaniac

e. Count Dracula

f. A still-life painter

g. An eccentric cat lady

(Answers on page 78)

Factoid

A Scottish chef surveyed 2000 UK families and found that most could produce seventy-two different meals just from combinations of the stuff they already had in the fridge!

PART TWO

THEORY

(or "science, psychology and other technical stuff about your fridge and you")

The Science of Fridge Magnets

Ever wonder how magnets are made? Or why they love your fridge door so much? Well, wonder no more! Those standard, annoying rubbery flat magnets that come with almost every pizza order are made with a magnetic powder (often iron rust) mixed with vinyl or plastic to make a wet substance scientifically known as goop. The goop is poured into a sheet mold and placed in a strong electromagnetic field. The north and south magnetic poles line up under the magnetic field and are locked in as the vinyl cools. The image is then printed on one side. The magnet sticks to your fridge's steel door because the magnetic field passes through the door from north to south poles.

Other more glitzy magnets (e.g., porcelain pigs, plastic sushi) with small iron bars or dots on the back are made either by cooling hot iron in an external magnetic field produced from an electric coil or by placing the iron next to other permanent magnets that transfer their magnetic force. The mini-magnet is then glued onto the object, packaged and sent to market.

Help! Why Won't My Magnets Stick?

We bet you have one of those fancy stainless steel, decorator-recommended refrigerators. Sadly, if the door contains more than two percent nickel (added for strength), you can kiss the magnetic force good-bye. But don't despair — there are other places you can showcase your artistic talents (see Beyond the Fridge on page 60).

Factoid

Neodymium magnets can hold up to one hundred times their weight. (They can also stop cardiac pacemakers, so keep Granny away from the fridge!)

A Web survey revealed that ...

42.9% of people say that fridge magnets shape their opinions of others.
(i.e., You can judge a book by its cover; a homeowner by his or her fridge.)

21.4% of people don't notice magnets at all.
(These types have their heads up in the clouds.)

25% of people find fridge magnets "irrelevant in a cold, heartless world."
(These people need to lighten up.)

3.6% of people feel they have no control over the magnets on their fridges.
(Things come and go and these people just passively sit there. They seem to think their fridge magnets are possessed.)
(They should pay a visit to Dr. Froid!)

4.3% of people have large magnet collections.
(And probably collect lots of other weird stuff, too.)

NORTHWINDS ELEMENTARY MEDIA CENTER
1111 7TH AVE NW
BUFFALO, MN 55313

The Psychological Meaning of Fridge Art

Introducing Dr. Henry Froid (pronounced "Freud")

In 1906, I received a diploma in psychology from the Correspondence School for the Non-Academically Inclined (Vienna campus). Upon graduation, I felt obliged to use my skills to help people improve their lives. I soon realized, however, that I was missing something. Nowhere in my training had I been taught to look at the refrigerator. Oh, sure, dream analysis has its place, but if you really want to understand someone's personality, as well as his or her unconscious wishes and desires, I advise you to look to the fridge. Fridge decoration can tell you everything you need to know — if only you know how to interpret what you see.

Let's begin with family relationships. You can tell how family members get along by looking at their fridge-decoration interaction. Is the effort harmonious and collaborative, or does one member dominate and control the refrigerator door? I once treated a man who posted so many pictures of himself with a large fish he had caught that he nudged his family's photos into the bottom right corner and then off altogether. Very distressing. A happy, well-balanced family's fridge door will exhibit equal amounts of each member's art and demonstrate obvious collaborative activity.

Fridge art can also show day-to-day psychological states: frustrations with school, chores, piano lessons and homework often leak onto the fridge in the form of angry newspaper clippings, hostile magnetic words and phrases or shocking images. I call this the "unconscious icebox" because you may not be aware of why certain pictures or decorations have been hung on the fridge, but dark feelings are nonetheless revealed in the choosing.

If you dig a little deeper, certain personality types can be detected by analyzing the fridge door. The narcissist's fridge is about "me, me, me." Narcissists display far too many pictures of their self-absorbed selves and they endlessly detail their achievements. They never show interest in others or the world at large. In contrast, people with low self-esteem use their refrigerators as a visual pep talk and confidence booster. Slogans, affirmations and goals all figure prominently.

Obsessive people can also be recognized by what's on their fridge. They are preoccupied with detail and control. Everything is arranged precisely, and themes and images are often displayed in sequence or by category. Woe befalls the person who dares move anything on *that* fridge!

Introverts and extroverts will have opposite fridge art styles. Introverts are shy and inhibited, and their fridges conceal more than they reveal. Extroverts, on the other hand, let it all hang out. You know who they are, what they like, who they love and where they want to go in life just from looking at their fridge doors.

You can even tell a right-brain person from a left-brain person based on their fridge decorations. You see, the brain is divided into two hemispheres — left and right — and one side predominates in each person. Left brainers are organized, verbal, logical and task oriented, and their fridges reflect this — minimal content presented in a sensible way. Right brainers are spontaneous, visual and creative, and their refrigerators veritably explode with chaos and color.

It's simply amazing the information you can amass from just a quick glance at a fridge door — and the decorators of the fridge probably don't even realize how revealing their art really is! Fascinating. (Feel free to rub your imaginary beard as you contemplate all of this.)

Introvert

Extrovert

Five Taboo Fridge Behaviors

(most often practiced by slightly immature males)

1. Dipping a finger in the strawberry jam

2. Drinking milk directly from the carton

3. Leaving less than half an inch of orange juice in the container

4. Licking the ice-cream lid

5. Squeezing chocolate syrup directly into the mouth

Factoid

November is Clean Out Your Refrigerator Month. Get busy!

Dr. Froid's Challenge: Your Turn

Now that you've had a crash course in fridge art psychoanalysis, it's time to put your new-found knowledge to work! How would you diagnose the following fridge-door *artistes* based on what they display? When you're finished your analysis, check out Dr. Froid's interpretations on the next page.

1. One hundred pie-eating contest ribbons

2. Thirty-three small magnetic clocks, all five minutes early

3. Wall-to-wall lottery tickets, scratch tickets, bingo cards and travel brochures on Timbuktu

4. Every rejection letter, e-mail or bad report card she has ever received from first grade on

5. Nothing but his baby teeth

Factoid

One enterprising artist has built a "Fridgehenge" installation near Los Alamos, New Mexico. It was set up to resemble Stonehenge, a mystical prehistoric stone monument in England.

Dr. Froid's Psychoanalysis:

1. This person is a compulsive carbohydrate consumer. He conceals his gluttonous urges by entering socially acceptable contests.

2. This person has obviously been traumatized at one point in her life for being late. Maybe she missed her wedding or final exams. Maybe she got fined for being five minutes late. She has vowed to never let this happen again but is now haunted by time.

3. This is a dreamer who longs for riches and escape. He wants to fall off the face of the earth never to be heard from again.

4. Pack your bags, we're going on a guilt trip! This Debbie Downer lives in the past and only sees the negative. Lighten up! Move on!

5. This somewhat creepy individual likes to hoard things and lacks a fantasy life. What kind of kid could have resisted the tooth fairy and the cash she leaves under the pillow? And what kind of adult keeps his baby teeth on display?

Quiz: What's on Your Fridge?

Check each item that appears on your fridge.

☐ receipts

☐ lists of chores

☐ pictures/family photos

☐ emergency phone numbers

☐ business cards

☐ lottery tickets

☐ nutrition tips

☐ appointment reminders

☐ take-out menus

☐ grocery lists

☐ bills

☐ homework reminders

If you checked two or more items, you have *Fridgeous Typicus*, a deadly boring refrigeration condition. To see how to cure this terrible ailment, read on …

PART THREE

PRACTICE

(or "nitty-gritty, get-your-hands-dirty and make some cool fridge art")

From FRIDGEOUS TYPICUS to FRIDGEOUS FABULOUS: An Insider's Guide

Now that you've learned the history, science and psychology of fridge art, how about learning how to make it? Here are some tips to get you started.

1. Let your imagination go crazy. Play with colors, textures, words and images. Dr. Froid would probably tell you crazy is bad. But his fridge is probably boring.

2. Be sure to buy fridge magnets in shops you visit and every time you travel someplace new. You might be inspired by one of them and create a cool new fridge display.

3. Leave out the boring stuff — go big or go home! Nobody wants to read a shopping list or class schedule. You should also try to avoid what I call Sibyl Snivel Syndrome — a fridge with nothing but history articles on it. Boring!

4. Follow your fascination. If it's sharks this month, go to town. If fluorescent skateboards turn your crank next, go for it! Why not have all magnets in the colors of your favorite sports team?

5. Pay attention to your dreams. (Why didn't Dr. Froid mention this? Isn't that what shrinks do?) Keep a record of nighttime images, places, colors and people, and make a dream scene on the fridge. You might want to leave out that weird bit with your math teacher and the tap dancing penguin, though. How would you explain that one?!

6. If you see a fridge concept you like somewhere, borrow it! Imitation is the sincerest form of flattery, after all.

7. Rivalry is healthy. Be sure to outdo all your friends and foes, and then rub their noses in it on a regular basis.

8. Change is good. Shake it up every couple of months by switching your fridge art for something new.

Factoid

Worldwide, guys prefer silver or black fridges, while girls prefer bright colors. White is still the number-one seller (and the best canvas for fridge art).

Finding Inspiration for Your Fridge Work

Fridge Feng Shui

Feng shui is Chinese for "wind-water" and it's the ancient practice of arranging objects to achieve harmony with the environment. Green or beige tones should point east. Red and purple, south. Steel or white, southwest. Black and blue, north. Buy a compass and be sure to point items inside and outside the fridge in the right direction based on color. For example, that jar of mystery sauce with the red label should face south — and don't forget to face all the tomatoes south, too! And, hey, if achieving harmony with the environment is not for you, you'll at least be confusing your family by moving stuff around.

A Word on TV Fridges

We all have our favorite TV shows and find inspiration for style and humor while watching them. Why not find ideas for your fridge there, too? Almost every episode of any show (cartoons included) has at least one kitchen scene. You may have to watch carefully, but you're certain to see magnets, pictures and objects on your favorite character's fridge, and you'll be able to tell whether he or she likes clutter or organization.

Take Cues from Nature

You never can tell when a new, brilliant visual concept will start percolating in your brain. Be observant and open-minded. Pay attention to flower patches, vegetable gardens, night skies, autumn trees, anthills, squashed rodents and cloud formations. Then use what you've seen to jump-start your creativity.

Getting Started:
101 Things to Hang on Your Fridge

1. acorns
2. advertisements
3. artificial flowers
4. baby rattles
5. balloons
6. cloth or metal badges
7. birthday and holiday cards
8. board game cards or play pieces
9. bottle caps
10. bows
11. bubble gum
12. buttons
13. candy hearts
14. CDs
15. ceramic tiles
16. clothes pegs
17. coins
18. comic strips
19. cupcake papers
20. cut-up illustrations from magazines
21. dice
22. dog biscuits
23. dominoes
24. drawings and paintings
25. dried flowers
26. dried pasta
27. drink cans
28. erasable message board
29. feathers
30. flower petals
31. foil paper
32. foil-wrapped candy
33. food labels
34. game-piece letters
35. gumdrops
36. hard candy
37. hockey pucks
38. holiday ornaments
39. jelly beans
40. jewelry
41. jigsaw puzzle pieces
42. keys (make sure no one needs them!)
43. kitchen timer
44. leaves
45. lipstick tubes
46. magazine covers
47. maps
48. marbles
49. matchboxes
50. melted wax globs
51. metal dog tags
52. mints in tins
53. movie posters
54. newspaper clippings
55. notepads
56. nuts in their shells
57. nuts and bolts
58. old book covers
59. old typewriter keys
60. origami
61. paper dolls
62. paper plates
63. party favors

64. pebbles and rocks
65. pencils and crayons
66. penny candy
67. photographs
68. picture frames
69. pinecones
70. pipe cleaners
71. placemats
72. plastic fruit and vegetables
73. play money
74. playing cards
75. pocket-sized dolls
76. poker chips
77. pom-pom critters
78. Popsicle sticks
79. postage stamps
80. postcards
81. recipe cards
82. record album covers
83. ribbons
84. seashells

85. seed packets
86. sheet music
87. small books
88. small candy and raisin boxes
89. small jars
90. spoons
91. sports cards
92. stickers
93. sunglasses
94. tickets
95. toothpaste tubes
96. toy cars
97. toy soldiers
98. twigs
99. watches
100. wooden letter blocks
101. yo-yos

Now use your imagination and come up with 101 more!

Five Things NOT to Hang on Your Fridge

1. Your neighbor's yappy Chihuahua
2. Your great-grandpa's toupee
3. Airplane barf bags
4. Toe jam/navel lint
5. Smelly socks

Fridge Art 101: Get Going with the Easiest Craft Project Ever

Almost any object can be turned into a fridge magnet in less than 30 seconds! This is so easy, your hamster could do it.

What you need:

- one small object — anything goes!

- one peel-and-stick magnetic dot or strip, available at dollar stores, office supply shops and craft supply stores

2. Remove the backing from the peel-and-stick magnetic strip or dot, and place the magnet on the back of the object, right in the center. If the object is a bit large or heavy, use two strips or dots.

3. Press firmly and leave for one hour.

What to do:

1. Make sure the back of the object you want to use is clean, dry and smooth.

4. Hang your new magnet proudly on your fridge. Ta-da!

Theme Fridge Masterpieces

You can totally wow your family by taking charge and decorating the fridge with seasonal, holiday or other select themes. Here's what to do (so they won't clobber you when you're done).

1. Get permission to decorate from the powers that be.

2. Put the stuff already on the fridge someplace safe. (You don't want Lucretia to forget when her root canal is, so don't lose her appointment card.)

3. Be careful with original photos. You can have free rein with pics that you scan or photocopy.

4. Invite suggestions or ask your family to collaborate on the project. Try to think outside the box. Halloween, Valentine's Day and Winter Fun fridges are fun, but wackier themes are even more fun. (See page 54 for tips on collaborating.)

5. Check out the theme examples that follow for inspiration.

6. Work fast before people change their minds.

The Birthday Fridge

This fridge will beat the pants off some boring balloons in the front yard. You will have to work under cover of night in order to surprise the birthday boy or girl!

Stuff you can use:

- embarrassing photos of the celebrant across his or her lifespan
- weird quotes and zippy images cut out from tabloid newspapers
- images of cakes, cupcakes and candles
- magnetic letters to spell out birthday wishes
- markers and cardboard
- balloons
- streamers and birthday hats

Some ideas:

1. Transform the fridge into a newspaper page, with images and text announcing the big day. Place photos and words in columns, like a real newspaper.

2. Make the fridge look like a huge birthday card.

3. Stick some party hats and streamers to the door.

4. Tie balloons to the door handle.

5. Put a cake with a message or punch line written on cardboard inside the fridge so that when it's opened there's a birthday surprise waiting!

6. Write a birthday message on the eggs with a marker.

Frame It!

Need a way to frame some birthday-related photos on the fridge? Try making some magnetic frames. They're cheap and easy to assemble, and they also make awesome gifts!

What you need:

- 21 cm (8½ in.) x 27.5 cm (11 in.) magnet sheet (available at craft supply stores)

- scissors, a ruler, a pencil

- craft knife*

- cutting mat

- paint (two colors)

- newspaper for protecting your work surface

- sponges or small paintbrushes

- stickers, fun fur, pom-poms or other decorations

*check with an adult before using

What to do:

1. Measure 6 cm (2½ in.) in from each side of the magnet sheet to create a rectangle in the middle of the sheet. Mark the lines in pencil and cut (with parental assistance), using the knife and a ruler to help you follow the lines.

2. Use the knife to shape the frame edges into scallops, curves or other designs, or leave them plain.

3. Paint your frame using paintbrushes or sponges, allowing each coat to dry before adding another one.

4. Jazz it up by adding stickers, fun fur, pom-poms or anything else that catches your eye.

The Brainwashing Fridge

Here's how to get the puppy you've always wanted but your parents keep saying no to. (You can use these ideas to obtain other expensive or forbidden items, as well. How about that state-of-the-art 89-gear mountain bike?) Think of it as subliminal advertising. Your fridge will wear them down until they say yes!

Stuff you can use:

- very cute pictures of the type of dog you want doing various cute things (frolicking, sitting, begging, making goo-goo eyes)

- pics of bones, balls, leashes, dog toys, etc.

- homemade magnetic words (see page 44) and thought bubbles (see page 79)

- erasable message board

- business cards of dog breeders, newspaper "dog for sale" ads, pictures of families and their dogs looking happy together

Some ideas:

1. Keep your eye out for suitable dog-related content and pictures in magazines and newspaper ads. Cut things out and file them away until you are ready to strike with your puppy campaign.

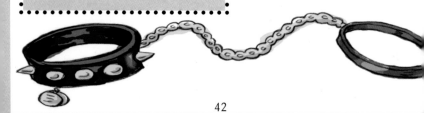

2. Put a big picture of you smiling on the fridge, surrounded by playful puppies. Tape up your photos from mags in a strategic fashion.

3. Make magnetic captions like "pets teach responsibility," "every child needs a dog," "pets lower blood pressure," "loyalty," "love" and "fetch." Sprinkle your captions around the photos.

4. Use the message board to rope people in with a "Name Our Dog Contest." (If they put down names, it means they have started to warm to your cause.)

5. Keep fine-tuning the fridge (and NAGGING) until you have Spot or Killer in your arms.

6. If you have access to a photo-editing program for your computer, take one of your family portraits, scan it and paste a photo of a puppy in it — as though it's already part of the family.

DAD'S TO-DO LIST
1. GET UP
2. RECEIVE HUG FROM
   LOVING CHILD
3. DRINK COFFEE
4. DRIVE TO DOG
   BREEDER
5. BUY PUPPY FOR
   LOVING CHILD AND
   RECEIVE HUGE HUG
6. DRIVE HOME
7. WATCH HAPPY CHILD
   PLAY WITH PUPPY

US AT NIAGARA FALLS

Letter Tiles

Here's another way to spell out your puppy-related desires. You can use either wooden letters from a Scrabble game or old computer keys (from a keyboard somebody threw out).

What you need:

- wooden letter tiles or computer keys removed from old keyboards

- peel-and-stick magnetic dots (one for each letter)

What to do:

1. Put a peel-and-stick magnetic dot on the back of all the letters from A to Z.

2. Place the letters randomly on the fridge, and see what words and brainwashing messages mysteriously appear!

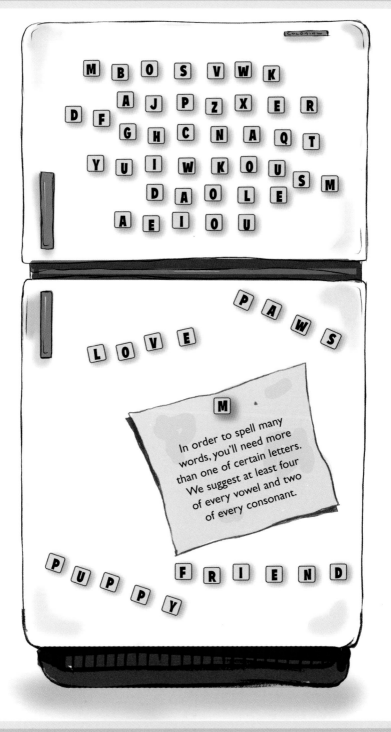

The "You'll Get Cavities!" Fridge

Putting colorful candy packages on the outside of the refrigerator makes for a catchy theme. More importantly, the candy has to be eaten first! A tough job, but I'm sure you can handle it. These magnets also make great (cheap!) gifts. Sweet!

What you need:

- small candy boxes (e.g., Halloween candy, raisins, metal mint tins)

- magnetic peel-and-stick strips or dots

What to do:

1. Open the boxes carefully, without damaging the cardboard.

2. Eat the contents of the boxes! This will make them empty and light — and your belly nice and full.

3. Stick the magnets to the back of the boxes, on the inside so that the magnets don't show. Or stick the magnets directly on the back of the boxes.

4. For metal mint tins, just throw a loose magnet inside with no glue because the magnet knows what to do.

5. Place boxes on top of the fridge (magnet side down) so that the magnetic force helps the adhesive to set.

6. Arrange boxes artistically on the fridge door. Feel free to eat more candy so you can add more boxes!

Dandy Candy Gem Magnets

Candy boxes not enough? Use some colorful wrappers to make these dazzle-ing magnets extra sweet!

ARE THOSE MAGNETS TASTY?

What you need:

- candy or gum wrappers

- scissors or craft knife*

- clear silicon glue (available at craft supply stores)

- scrap paper (white or light colored)

- toothpicks

- large flat-bottomed glass gems (available at craft stores)

- peel-and-stick magnetic dots

- newspaper for protecting your work surface

- optional: craft hole punch, glitter, markers (to make your own images)

*check with an adult before using

What to do:

1. Place the gem over your chosen image and trace around it.

2. Use scissors, a craft knife or a craft hole punch to cut around the circle you've traced.

3. Glue the picture you've cut to scrap paper and allow the glue to dry. Cut around the picture. The extra layer of paper will prevent the magnet from showing through.

4. Squirt some glue onto another scrap of paper and then use a toothpick to scoop up a pea-sized blob. Dab the glue onto your cut-out picture, right side up.

5. Lower the gem onto the glue and press gently. Work quickly to make sure that the glue doesn't begin to set before your picture is in place — but carefully so you don't crumple the picture.

6. Allow the glue to dry, gem-side down, picture side up. Once dry, peel and stick the magnetic dot to the back of the picture.

The Fridge of Horror

This design is great for Halloween, Friday the Thirteenth or any other date you feel requires some honest-to-goodness, blood-chilling terror (e.g., your sister's sweet 16?).

Stuff you can use:

• unattractive photos of family members just waking up

• photos, postcards and drawings of other sinister things: ghosts, demons, skulls, witches, zombies, vampires, movie monsters, gargoyles, tombstones, UFOs, aliens, ravens, rats, cockroaches, screaming people, your geography teacher, bloody body parts, etc.

• creepy magnets (e.g., skulls and black cats — often available in dollar stores at Halloween)

• homemade magnetic words and thought bubbles (see page 44 and page 79). Examples: "Boo!" "Take me to your leader." "I want to suck your blood."

• fake cobwebs and wash-off blood (available at party, costume and dollar stores)

• colored lightbulbs

Some ideas:

1. Identify phobias your family members have (e.g., snakes) and make sure to use lots of these images in your design.

2. Pick images or recreate scenes from family-favorite horror movies.

3. Clip or tape pics and use with magnetic words (see page 52) to tell a story. (e.g., "This is what happened when Dad turned into a demon …")

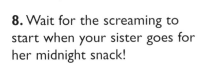

8. Wait for the screaming to start when your sister goes for her midnight snack!

4. Does Aunt Lucy resemble the Bride of Frankenstein? Then juxtapose their two photos in a funny way. Or put Auntie's head on Bridie's body.

5. Smear wash-off blood (or ketchup) in between photos (and on them, if they are extra copies).

6. Spray on cobwebs.

7. Change the kitchen lightbulb to red, black or orange for added drama.

Dark and Stormy Night Word Sets

Get your family's scary juices flowing with these creepy story starters.

What you need:

- white flat magnetic strips or magnet sheets
- scissors or craft knife*
- ruler
- fine-tipped marker

*check with an adult before using

2. If your parents agree, go on-line to find some word lists. You'll need a good variety of words as well as lots of simple ones, like "the," "and," "but" and so on.

3. Using a marker, neatly write out the words and sentences on the strips of magnet, then cut the strips into individual pieces.

What to do:

1. Have a look at some of your favorite ghost stories for inspiration and come up with some spooky sentences. Examples: "It was a dark and stormy night." "She heard a noise downstairs." "The wind howled in the trees." "The killer had escaped from jail."

The thunder roared.

Her head fell off with a thump

It rolled across the creaking floo

Her mother screamed, "Finish your homework!"

4. Place all the sentences and joining words on the fridge to create some spook-tacular ghost stories.

5. You might want to include some blank strips and a marker on a string, too, so that you can add words as the story takes shape.

Interact with Your Fridge – and Each Other

"An empty fridge, inside or out, is the sign of a misspent life."
— Martha Stew-Pot, media maven

The fridge can be more than just a blank canvas for your artistic side. It can also be a way to do things with your family when you don't actually have time to get together.

How about this: put store-bought or homemade word magnets up on the fridge. Scatter them randomly or group them according to type (nouns, verbs, adjectives, adverbs). Explain that each member gets to compose one full line of a poem until there are no more words or fridge space, or the poem seems done.

People can take as long as they want — it will be a nice surprise when you go to the fridge and see that Mom has finally finished her poem line. (Not such a nice surprise to find leftover brussels sprouts in the fridge.)

Below is an example of a family fridge poem. It's terrible. I'm sure you can do better!

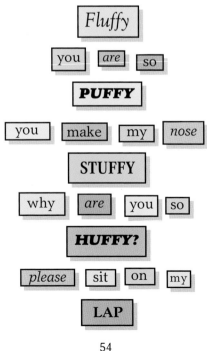

Another way to have fridge-related family activity is to stick on a wipe board and some markers and have long-running games. Hangman and tic-tac-toe work well. Or find a magnetic checkers set and draw the board yourself. What about cutting crossword puzzles out of the newspaper? You could even post weekly riddles or trivia on the fridge and challenge each other to get the answer. The fridge as a competitive arena — why hasn't anyone thought of that before?!

Sample Fun Family Quiz

Take turns drawing each other's brains on the wipe board and guess which brain belongs to which person. Could this be your big brother's brain?

More Family Bonding:
Magnetic Greeting Cards

Family far away? You can still keep in touch via the fridge with these magnetic greeting cards.

What to do:

1. Choose photos that will be easy to crop and have clear definition around the people or objects.

2. If your photos are not digital or you are using a combination of photos and illustrations, scan them to your computer.

3. Using the "freehand" tool in your photo-editing program, trace the image you'd like to use. Then copy and paste the image into a new photo document. (Make sure the new document has the dimensions 21 cm (8½ in.) x 27.5 cm (11 in.), so that it matches the size of the magnet sheet.)

4. Repeat step 3 until you have created your new image. Add the greeting at the top.

Good Luck in your First Game!

5. Now you are ready to print. Do a test print on regular paper before using a magnet sheet. Make any adjustments to the size, layout or dimensions.

6. Ask your big sister or parental unit to help you. Load the magnet sheet into your printer according to the package directions, and then print away!

7. Using scissors or a craft knife, carefully cut out the greeting card and trim the edges to remove any white border or to create a fancy border.

Cool Alternative

If you don't have access to a photo-editing program or to a computer geek who has one, you can go to the photography store or photo department at most chain stores and they can produce photo-magnets for you, for a fee.

The Cartoon Strip Fridge

Here's a way to turn your fridge door into a super-sized comic book or funnies page.

Stuff you can use:

- cut out comic strips from different sources (black-and-white or color)

- pictures of family members

- homemade magnetic thought bubbles (see page 79)

- clear tape

- magnetic peel-and-stick strips or dots

- small superhero action figures

2. Place the comic strips in a sequence that tells a short story, like the comics page in your newspaper.

3. Using clear tape on the back, add photos of family members with funny thought bubbles above their heads. Make them part of the story. (e.g., "Here comes Super-Mom!")

4. Put a magnetic dot on the back of a small toy action figure and have him or her point proudly to your masterpiece!

Some ideas:

1. Take the comic strips to your local print or photocopy store and ask them to enlarge the images (or fiddle with the photocopier in the school library). You can also get them laminated at your local stationery store if you want. Then put peel-and-stick magnetic strips or dots on the backs.

Eleven Little-Known Bizarre Holiday Fridge Themes

Use these weirdo dates to inspire fridge designs nobody else on your block will think of in a million years.

January 2	Squirrel Appreciation Day
March 1	Lost Sock Memorial Day
April 2	Peanut Butter and Jelly Day
April 25	World Penguin Day
May 9	National Junk Food Day
June 23	All Pink Day
July 21	Love-a-Pig Day
August 18	Bad Poetry Day
October 9	Moldy Cheese Day
November 4	King Tut Day
December 7	National Cotton Candy Day

Why stop here? Make even more bizarre festive days. How about

• Yellow Teeth Day • Drool Appreciation Day
• Saltine Cracker Day • Count Your Zits Day
• Two-Ply Toilet Tissue Day

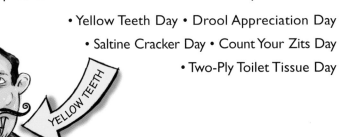

YELLOW TEETH

59

Beyond the Fridge

By now your fridge might be getting a bit crowded. If you can't find room for even one more rubber chicken on there, don't despair ... expand! Try these suggestions for where to put your magnets and pics when your fridge door is just too full.

Take those cookie sheets out of the cupboard and decorate them. (Just remember to remove all the magnets before baking cookies.)

Brighten your postal delivery person's day by decorating your mailbox.

Take your mother's mind off her taxes by decorating the filing cabinet in her office.

Don't forget your school locker — it *is* kind of fridge-shaped, isn't it?

"I would never have become a successful artist if I hadn't started fiddling with our fridge when I was six years old. I think my parents sent me to art school so they could eat. I was always blocking access to the food in the refrigerator when I was in the throes of inspiration."

— Ice Grrrl, It-Girl of the Art Scene

Do Not Try This!

Worst Fridge Magnet Project Ever

While researching this book, the author encountered a step-by-step project for making a magnetic furry cat bum with its tail in the air … No, we will NOT provide the instructions here!

Quiz: What's Your Entrepreneurial Quotient?

(That's EQ for Short)

1. You spot a nickel on the sidewalk. What do you do?

a. Pick it up and put it in your pocket. As your granddad always says, "A penny saved is a penny earned."

b. Give it to a young neighbor and say, "Here, kid. Buy yourself some candy," then walk away chuckling at the thought of how mad the kid will be when he discovers he can't actually buy anything for a nickel.

c. Just keep right on walking. You have a big meeting with *Tycoons Today* magazine, and you can't afford to stop for a lousy nickel.

2. You have a big order for magnets and a school project — both due tomorrow. What do you do?

a. Explain to your customer that your schoolwork always comes first, and tell her she'll get her magnets next week.

b. Fill the magnet order and ditch the homework — no one will care about an F on your record once you're a kazillionaire.

c. Hire a young neighbor (although perhaps not the one from 1b. above), and set him to work cranking out magnets. The secret to success is knowing when to delegate.

3. Your friends have complained that you never have time to see them now that you have started your own business. How do you respond?

a. You realize they are right and that friends should always come before money. You take a few days off to hang out with the gang.

b. You realize they are right but decide that once you've made your first million, you'll be able to buy all new friends — better friends.

c. You realize they are right. So you hire them for a pittance. Now you get to hang out together, and they are helping you to prosper at the same time.

(Answers on page 78)

PART FOUR

BUSINESS

(or "and now for some ways to make cold hard cash and become a business whiz")

Fridge Design for Fun and Profit

Business Tips from Donald Grump, CEO, None of Your Beeswax Inc.

An empty fridge door is not a blank canvas — it's a gold mine! Just picture all the fridges in the world, each one covered in magnets. Who's churning out those magnets? Someone who's laughing all the way to the bank, that's who! So get off that couch and get to work.

A (Grumpy) Factoid

It did not take long before some smarty-pants in the corporate world saw the potential of the refrigerator as a product-billboard in every North American home. (Wish I'd thought of it first!) Magnet Inc. was founded in the early 1980s by Bill Wood of Washington, Missouri, and is currently the leading maker of specialty ad-magnets in the world, producing custom products for Pizza Hut, Ford, GM, Holiday Inn and hundreds of other big companies. His Canadian counterpart and number two in sales is Simple Signman, founded in Chambly, Quebec, by Len Dunshire.

Setting Up Your Own Fridge Magnet Business

by Donald Grump, CEO

Here's an eight-step business plan to get you going. And I mean it. Get going before somebody else does!

1. Research the competition. Check out magnets in every gift shop, dollar store, stationery store and craft fair you visit.

2. Pick a target audience. Who do you want to buy your product? Kids, adults, males, females, business people? All of the above?

3. Decide what kinds of magnets you want to produce. Come up with something original. Or if that fails, try the ideas in the Practice section.

4. Set short-term goals (e.g., supplementing your allowance). Then contemplate long-term goals (e.g., becoming a fridge magnet billionaire within three years).

5. Decide on unit pricing. For example, figure out how much it costs to produce one mini-raisin-box magnet. Can you buy raisin boxes in bulk at Halloween and sell the actual raisins to Aunt Ida, who makes raisin pie? Who has the cheapest peel-and-stick magnetic dots? (Check craft stores and Web sites.) Then charge a little bit more than it costs you for materials, so that you make a profit. (Isn't business fun?)

6. Develop a marketing strategy. You'll probably begin selling by word of mouth and to family, and then by hitting up classmates. Then start an e-mail campaign, if your parents give the okay. Talk to a family member who is in business for more ideas.

7. Look at channels of distribution. Do you want to hit school craft shows? How about rummage sales? Garage sales? Will you start mailing products to friends and family who live far away? Do you know the lady who owns the local gift shop? Can you get friends to sell products for a small commission? Do you want to sell your magnets on-line?

8. Keep track of costs, expenses, lost or "borrowed" product, unpaid bills, etc. Count your profits and revisit your business plan every year to keep on track. Prepare for world domination!

Go Big or Go Home:
How to Make a Name as a Fridge Artist

First you have to actually decorate a fridge or two. Then you can start sharing your talents with others. Maybe they'll even pay you. And if they don't, well, at least you won't starve. (Just open the fridge door when hunger strikes.) Here's how you can guide others into the wild world of fridge art:

Always carry photos of your past creations. E-mail images and updates regularly to potential clients.

Leave your business card attached to your own fridge. Even better, make fridge magnets with your name and phone number on them. Hand them out to people you know. Even if they don't hire you, they might call you up sometime just to chat.

Ask potential clients about their preferences for color, theme, clutter versus simplicity, and good taste versus the height of grossness.

If someone hires you to do a fridge for a special occasion, suggest to them that ideally their fridge will receive constant updating, which you are willing to do — for a fee!

Let people know you will make house calls. That's right! They don't have to drop their fridges off for decorating. You'll actually go to them. What a deal!

Expand your services to decorating locker doors, dorm-room mini-fridges and basement freezers.

Show potential clients this book. Then they will know that your work is totally cutting edge.

Fridge Art for Charity

Work with your class to make some cash for a good cause. How about making a fridge art calendar?

Talk to your art teacher about the idea so that your school lends support and credibility to the project.

Decide as a class what charity you want to support and then inform it of your idea.

Here's the plan. Have your classmates decorate their fridges with different monthly themes. They can take a photo of their decorated fridge and then e-mail it to an address set up by your teacher. Specify a deadline and stick to it!

Select images for each month, keeping in mind that some images will suit specific seasons or dates. (No Santa images in July, please!)

Decide as a committee how you want the calendar to look. Make sure the artists are given credit and that the charity and your school are highlighted big-time in the final product.

Talk to your teacher about production methods. Can the work be scanned at school? Does your teacher have a computer program for calendar design, or do you need to price production at a photo or stationery store? Is there a school art budget for activities like this, or do you need donations (or advance sales) to get the project off the ground?

Decide on a price.

Ask your classmates how many calendars each of them can realistically sell and what your target goal for the charity will be. This will help you decide how many calendars to print.

The project should be ready to sell for November so that you can maximize seasonal gift-giving!

Design an official-looking envelope for collecting funds, and have the teacher hold onto the proceeds for safe-keeping.

If the project goes well, your school may keep sponsoring it for years to come. That would be a real help to the charity you've chosen to support.

ADVANCED FRIDGE ART:
What Some Brave Souls Have Actually Done (from Wallpaper to Graffiti)

Many icebox artists the world over have moved beyond basic fridge collage techniques or magnet-loading and have tried some pretty wacky things! We're talking Fridgeus Outrageous! Here are some real (but crazy) examples. But don't, and I mean DON'T, try these at home! Disaster could ensue.

In extensive travel researching this book, we've come across:

• a company in Alberta that will turn your fridge into a "faux" gas pump, vault safe or power-chopper motorcycle!

• a British company that sells brightly colored Union Jack fridges all ready to go

YES, BUT IS IT FRIDGE ART?

- one fridge with foreign coins permanently glued onto it, another with nothing but pink pigs and yet another with decapitated "teen fashion doll" heads (paging Dr. Froid!)

- a designer who wallpapered the fridge to match the kitchen walls

- a night sky fridge painted black with glow-in-the-dark stars, and an aquarium fridge painted turquoise with magnetic fish

- an artist who lets people write graffiti on the fridge with erasable markers whenever they come to visit

- an abandoned fridge recycled into a bookshelf, and another into a coffee table

There is clearly no end to fridge-a-licious creativity. What would YOU do to the family fridge if given carte blanche by the powers that be?

Draw a sketch. Then dream of the day you have your own apartment ...

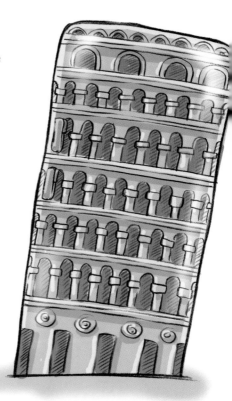

"Fridge magnets are hideous and should be banned altogether. If you want to be an artist, go to art school."
— Andy Warthog, avant-garde-ist

Your Final Fridge Art Questions Answered

Q: Is fridge art addictive?
A: Definitely. There is no turning back once you begin, but the risks are few.

Q: Is there anything that can't go on the fridge?
A: Probably not. If you can stick it on and it doesn't object, go ahead! This includes living things. One lady grew plants in small square pots and stuck them to her fridge. Of course, cats and dogs are another story ...

Q: Any potential health risks from electromagnetic waves if I put a lot of magnets on my refrigerator?
A: None, but watch out for tipping fridges!

Q: How often should I change my fridge art?
A: Daily, weekly, monthly or yearly. It all depends on you. Follow your bliss!

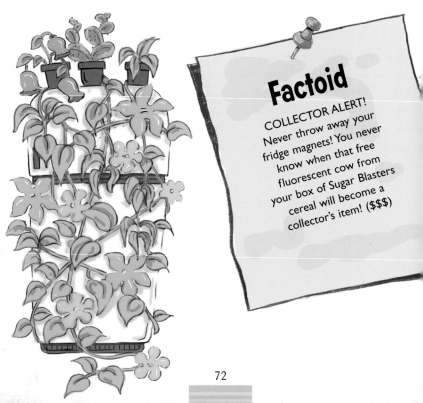

Factoid

COLLECTOR ALERT! Never throw away your fridge magnets! You never know when that free fluorescent cow from your box of Sugar Blasters cereal will become a collector's item! ($$$)

Q: Every time people come over to our house, they rearrange my magnets and fiddle with the decorations and photos. Don't they understand this is art?

A: Would they repaint the Mona Lisa? Alas, to be great is to be misunderstood. Be assertive. Put up a magnetic sign: "Don't touch or you are ground beef!"

Q: Why would a grown-up decorate the fridge? Why not let us kids do it?

A: Most adults have frustrated artistic urges. Many would like to play an instrument or write poetry but don't have the talent, time or equipment. Fridge art costs little and allows the creative juices to flow. Besides, grown-ups desperately miss finger painting and art class!

Q: Has fridge art ever been exhibited?

A: Yes, especially in New York City, where people tend to be pretty eccentric to begin with. Generally, the art is displayed on real fridge doors from discarded refrigerators and suspended from the ceiling.

Q: I'm running out of room … what now?!

A: Try hanging cookie sheets in the kitchen or decorating your locker, filing cabinets or the garage door. Does anyone in the family have a metal plate in his or her head?

Q: Our landlord thinks we're strange. I see it in his eyes when he goes in our kitchen. What should we do?

A: Give him this book, and tell him that a bodacious fridge can only enhance his property value.

The Future of Fridge Art

From Smart Magnets to the Virtual Refrigerator

We've seen how fridge art began in prehistoric caves, moved on to ice rooms and wooden iceboxes and finally to the adorned modern metal refrigerator. And now fridge art has even gone virtual. On-line opportunities are endless! If your parents are okay with it, you can now find Web sites where you can move "letter magnets" around to spell words.

Other sites allow you to post notes and artwork. You can post images of your fridge magnet collections, magnetic poems, decorated theme fridges or family projects. There are sites dedicated to "refrigerator graveyards" for discarded, forlorn appliances. Some people even use Web cameras to document what's INSIDE the fridge. Way weird!

Appliance companies are trying to outdo each other with new bells and whistles: video and computer screens built into the door, elaborate messaging systems and e-mail capabilities, faux aquariums and diet-coach voices that scold you every time you open the door. You can now send photos from your cell phone to your fridge door! Researchers at the Viktoria Institute in Sweden have even developed "intelligent fridge magnets." Each magnet has a 6-character liquid crystal display and can randomly generate a word, and then classify it as a noun, verb, adjective, adverb, conjunction or article. The magnets can then be "trained" to communicate with each other to form grammatically correct sentences or even to write poetry. You just shake them and they start over.

Who knows where the once humble refrigerator will go — and what it will look like in the future? But I think it's safe to say that wherever the fridge goes, fabulous art will follow!

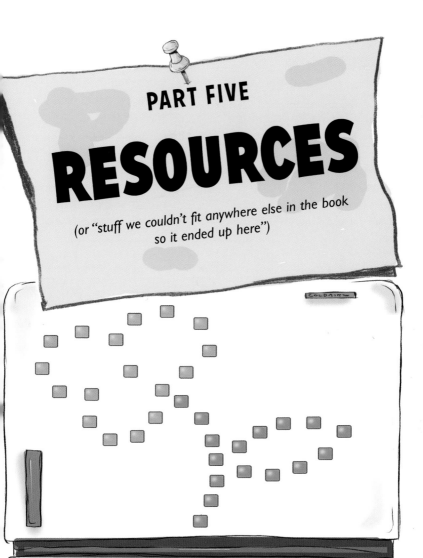

PART FIVE

RESOURCES

(or "stuff we couldn't fit anywhere else in the book so it ended up here")

Organize Those Magnets!
Most people throw magnets on the fridge willy-nilly. Why not use magnetic letters to make a flower with all A's for the stem, Z's for the petals and X's for the leaves? How about an orange flame shape or a blue-and-white tsunami? Or make big letters out of small word tiles to spell "You Stink!"

Quiz Answers

Celebrity Fridges
Answers: 1b, 2c, 3e, 4d, 5a

What's Inside Your Fridge?
Answers: 1e, 2a, 3f, 4b, 5g, 6c, 7d

What's Your Entrepreneurial Quotient?
Scoring: If you answered mostly a's, you are a nice guy. And we all know where they finish. If you answered mostly b's, you are definitely not a nice guy. You might have the right entrepreneurial spirit, but people just don't like you. If you answered mostly c's — congratulations! You have everything you need to be a successful entrepreneur!

Try This!

The following can be used to affix objects to your refrigerator door:

- clear tape

- duct tape (if you have permission and want to make sure no one removes what's there)

- magnetic clips

- sticky putty

- homemade or store-bought magnets (including unadorned black metal dots)

- magnetic picture frames

- chewing gum (a temporary solution only)

Magnetic Hang-Ups
- Apply a peel-and-stick magnetic strip (found at craft supply stores) to the back of a clothespeg for an instant clip.
- Take a piece of flat cork and stick a peel-and-stick magnetic dot to the back. You can now use thumbtacks and turn your fridge into a bulletin board.
- Cut a pencil-thin strip from a 21 cm ($8^{1}/_{2}$ in.) x 27.5 cm (11 in.) magnet sheet (found in craft supply stores). Decorate as you see fit. You can then hang several photos at once, vertically, horizontally or willy-nilly.

Secrets of the Cartoon Thought Bubble

1. Buy a white magnet sheet at a craft supply or stationery store.

2. Using the picture below as a guide, draw some bubbles and cut them out. (Nail scissors make nice clean edges.)

3. Use erasable markers to write funky or embarrassing sentences, or to have people in the photos "talk" to each other.

4. Place strategically over the heads of your subjects.

Examples:

Magnet Recycling for Cheapskates

Why buy new magnetic backing when you can recycle the free ones? You can cut them up, paint them, glue them to the backs of cards and photos, or plaster them with stickers, feathers or fabric.

If the square magnet from Joe's Pizza is starting to look a bit tired, here's what you can do: choose an image from a magazine or old picture book (maybe not your little sister's favorite!). Put the magnet over the image you want to use and outline it, adding an extra half-inch all the way around. Cut out the image. Glue it over the magnet, folding and sticking the extra half-inch of paper behind the magnet. Isn't that better than looking at someone else's advertising? Or if ads are okay with you, at least glue your own ad on there.

Cut It Out!

• Draw small wacky hats on blank white magnet sheets. Color them with markers and then place them selectively above heads in photos.

• Why stop at hats? Blow up a photo of someone and make far-out cut-out magnetic clothes. Dad will love that purple polka-dot psychedelic tie!

A Word on Store-Bought Magnets

There are currently thousands of decorative fridge magnets available in shops and craft supply stores around the world. But after reading this book, you know that there is *nothing* in a store that you can't make better yourself. Nothing store-bought can match that fuzzy feeling you get inside after putting your cat's head on a movie star's body and carefully placing a magnetic strip on the back. Just try it and see!